ANNABEL HOWLAND

HENNA NADEEM

INGRID POLLARD

CAMILA SPOSATI

THE SEARCH FOR TERRESTRIAL
INTELLIGENCE (S.T.I. CONSORTIUM)

Landscape
Trauma
in the age of scopophilia

AUTOGRAPH
ABP

an Autograph exhibition
curated by Richard Hylton

Published for the exhibition:
LANDSCAPE TRAUMA IN THE AGE OF SCOPOPHILIA

thegallery & Dilston Grove,
Southwark Park, London,
4 July–5 August 2001

Leeds Metropolitan University Gallery, Leeds,
9 November–15 December 2001

LANDSCAPE TRAUMA IN THE AGE OF SCOPOPHILIA
was an Autograph touring exhibition curated by
Richard Hylton, assisted by Jananne Al-Ani.

The exhibition and publication were produced
with funds from The National Lottery Touring
Programme at the Arts Council of England,
London Arts and the Mondriaan Foundation.

Edited by Richard Hylton, assisted by Jananne Al-Ani
Editorial Clair Joy

TEXTS © 2001 Jorella Andrews and Richard Hylton
WORKS © the Artists
PHOTOGRAPHY © 2001 Autograph and the Artists

All dimensions are height × width.

Published in the United Kingdom by Autograph –
The Association of Black Photographers (abp),
London 2001.

Autograph (abp)
74 Great Eastern Street,
London EC2A 3JG

info@ auto.demon.co.uk
www.autograph-abp.co.uk

DESIGN Eugenie Dodd Typographics
PHOTOGRAPHY Peter Barker
PRINTING Burlington Press
COVER IMAGE Camila Sposati, Talk to Me, 2000

A catalogue record of this book is available from
the British Library.

ISBN 1 899282 80 7

Why a show on landscape? What could be so traumatic about the landscape? Over the past year significant climatic changes have brought unprecedented rainfalls and floods, causing national rail disruption and bringing Britain to a virtual standstill. Furthermore, the countryside has been experiencing a seemingly never-ending industrial and agricultural crisis typified by the spread of disease through livestock. Cities across Britain have been caught in the ever-spiraling rise in the cost of living, symbolized by the insatiable drive of redevelopment and gentrification. Arguably, globalization is the backdrop, if not the cause, of many of these ills. This has produced a climate of uncertainty across the ecological, political, economic and cultural terrain. Arguments over the autonomy of the countryside continue to simmer, whilst the growth of brownfield sites is measured by the proportionate decline in greenfield sites. Internationally, the right to own and roam is questioned as in the violent farmland disputes in Zimbabwe. All of this is part of the answer to my initial question.

However, there is also a more specific reason why I wanted to curate the exhibition LANDSCAPE TRAUMA. For this project brings me back, albeit it in a different way, to that unfashionable and equally loaded issue of identity, an issue that has played a role in some of my previous curatorial projects. In 1992 I curated an exhibition called SHIFTING BORDERS,[1] which asked the question: What Does Europe Mean to You? The exhibition focused on examining "the parameters of personal cultural belonging, questioning how far they will shift in a fluid social, economic and geographical climate".[2] Coinciding with Britain's first Presidency of the European Community, the exhibition was about how the subject of Europe could inflame radically opposing opinions. For some, a United States of Europe threatened national sovereignty, whilst for others it symbolized a citadel of xenophobia. Some four years later I curated the exhibition IMAGINED COMMUNITIES (1996)[3] which explored the meaning and mythology of community. SHIFTING BORDERS explored the macro-politics of identity as manifested in the nation state. IMAGINED COMMUNITIES explored the question of belonging by looking at the micro-politics of nation, namely local communities. The exhibition argued that:

> "Despite, or because of, the divisiveness of [Thatcherism], people began to question openly, the notion that communities fall into neat categories . . . not only could we no longer make assumptions about what exists across different communities, but also we cannot assume to know what exists within them."[4]

What linked these two exhibitions was a desire to consider 'identity' through ideas about nation and community, ideas that are integral to a differentiated society. This is an important point today for how often are questions of identity aired in a tone that presumes some already determined status quo that exists beyond question and explanation?

SHIFTING BORDERS and IMAGINED COMMUNITIES considered political and cultural terrain through the spectacle of the subject. The photographic, digital and video work in LANDSCAPE TRAUMA considers a terrain vacated by a figurative subject, approaching the question of identity from a different trajectory: not from the subject, but from the self. In his essay, 'The Gaze in the Expanded Field', Norman Bryson scrutinizes the assumptions of the Cartesian model for looking, in which "the subject conceives of itself as universal centre, surrounded by the stable plenitude of an object world".[5] Although this perspectival terrain offers a profound sense of stability, unseen mechanisms of power are at play within its structure. Bryson points out that, through viewing, we enter into terrain in which sight equals perception, far from being natural, it is socially created and imbued with a "politics of vision". What interests me about Bryson's critique is that it raises questions not only about the political implications for how we see the world but also questions our position within it.

Using landscape as a common starting point, the artists in LANDSCAPE TRAUMA present illusions of scale, space and time which, through processes of construction, destruction and reconfiguration, disrupt the familiar picture plane. The disorienting effects intend to provoke a reconsideration of the relationships and assumptions associated with the act of looking.

Henna Nadeem's collages are assembled from generic photographs of nature commonly found in calendars or magazines like NATIONAL GEOGRAPHIC. Given their ubiquity, these are the sort of images which one might ordinarily pay little attention to. However, Nadeem rejuvenates these somewhat clichéd depictions of nature through a process which is both meticulous and quite unassuming. Reminiscent of Vermeer's paintings which have double perspectives, making it difficult for our eyes to settle, Nadeem's collages force our eyes to flit between the whole and the skeletal duplicate which is overlaid. To take on board the coherent whole means seeing the fractured surface; viewing the fractured surface means we cannot see the whole. This continual shifting of focus becomes a metaphor for the presence of another viewer and, by implication, perhaps a different view.

The relatively low tech but labour intensive nature of Nadeem's collages is similar to the process used by **Annabel Howland**. Armed with a scalpel, Howland cuts away the pictorial co-ordinates of the photographs she has taken and enlarged. Consequently, these images become quite disorienting, existing as they do on the threshold of abstraction. In ROADLINES I (2000) the iconic image of the American Highway, made so familiar by Hollywood, becomes a terrain distinguished as much by what is not there, as by what remains. What was on the horizon? A mountain range? More endless highway? We can only imagine. Resonances occur between pictorial space and the physicality of the photograph. Where skid marks in the pictorial distance portray a scene captured by camera, marks more typical of painting than photography represent the residual effects of meticulous cutting. Howland understands the fragility of identity as representation, and extends this to the fragile anatomical structure of her works. For what remains uncut hangs from the wall in a precarious corporeal state, reliant on its fastenings for physical and pictorial coherence.

Where Howland's cutting and Nadeem's assemblages are employed to disrupt the picture plane, TALK TO ME (2000) by **Camila Sposati** uses filmic editing and scripting devices to produce a fragmented moment. A visual and aural conundrum, TALK TO ME questions the certainty of time and space, intimacy and dislocation. Beginning with an awesome aerial view of a metropolis, fragmented dialogue becomes the focus of our attention; moments of communion are undone by discordant responses. What is so powerful about this piece is the subtle interplay between what we see and what we hear. A conversation about the past, present and future swings from fantasy to indifference while the roving camera also becomes a kind of lost spirit, moving continuously, through night to day. Circling the traces of life below, the camera's gaze remains perpetually distant and dislocated.

A significant part of **Ingrid Pollard**'s photographic practice over the years has been her concern with the countryside as the locus for identity. For LANDSCAPE TRAUMA, Pollard's images represent a departure from a figurative mode of working. Honing in on the minutiae of the land, these images initially look like representations of geological forms. Yet, having undergone a process of enlargement, they become images of landscapes within landscapes reminiscent of some of Blake's work or even the apocalyptic world of Hieronymus Bosch, minus the figures. By inverting the micro and the macro, Pollard invokes a kind of irony, inasmuch as getting closer to nature produces a Pandora's box of representation. Where Howland illuminates the fragility of identity through its proximity to abstraction, Pollard uses abstraction for its potential to mobilise the infinite and equally troubled terrain of the imaginary.

The relation between the psychic and the scientific is critical to this exhibition because, in an age of technology, the authority of the eye is increasingly being displaced by a reliance on autonomous systems to do our seeing for us. As far back as 1976 a space probe named Viking Orbiter was sent to Mars and relayed blurred images to earth which revealed little to the naked eye. However, after some digital processing the indistinct shapes unveiled something resembling a face. Although by contemporary standards the results were rather crude, this example of space exploration's tendency toward anthropomorphism is at the heart of **The Search for Terrestrial Intelligence**'s (S.T.I.) interactive website project.[6] The interactive nature of this project aims to draw attention to our role as viewers in producing meaning from images.

Inviting the participant to locate signs of terrestrial life by selecting a location on an aerial photograph, S.T.I. engages the viewer in a pseudo-scientific experiment in which data is gathered and processed. S.T.I. draws on the populist fascination with alien life as portrayed in the THE X-FILES or the film 2001: A SPACE ODYSSEY. However, while Hal, the talking computer from 2001: A SPACE ODYSSEY undermines human endeavour, signaling the possible autonomy of the computer, S.T.I. reminds us that technology is often used as a way to maintain already existing social, political and cultural relations.

A question frequently asked during the production of this exhibition was, why the title LANDSCAPE TRAUMA IN THE AGE OF SCOPOPHILIA? Given that the spectacle of trauma is played out indefatigably in photography and television, it seems appropriate to question the possibly disturbing relationship between subject and viewer. For what does it mean to be fed a daily ration of war, starvation and genocide? From terror to celebrity, the power of the media turns representation on itself – the repetition of images becomes a kind of cannibalism where subjects are dehumanised. As Bryson says, what is most troubling about sight is not simply the horror of what we might see but its power to "naturalize terror, and that is of course what is terrifying".[7] As spectators, we have grown accustomed to a Western culture based on "image feedback", an abstracted 'reality' that is really about producing money and focusing opinion. Yet, far from circumventing the spectacular, LANDSCAPE TRAUMA IN THE AGE OF SCOPOPHILIA is obsessed with images which are both extraordinary and relentlessly engaging. Perhaps this is the perversity and ambiguity of the show. For can one really deny the sheer pleasure, and authority, afforded by the spectacle of looking? The work in this exhibition however recognizes the value in destabilizing this authority. Not simply by replacing a stable view with a fragmented one, but by seeing them as positions inextricably connected and worth troubling.

Richard Hylton CURATOR September 2001

1 SHIFTING BORDERS: WHAT DOES EUROPE MEAN TO YOU? Laing Art Gallery, Newcastle-Upon-Tyne, 20 August–18 October 1992.

2 SHIFTING BORDERS, Press Pack, 1992.

3 IMAGINED COMMUNITIES A National Touring Exhibition organized by the Hayward Gallery, London in collaboration with Oldham Art Gallery, 27 January–24 March 1996.

4 Richard Hylton, 'I said, I am that I am, I am, I am, I am', IMAGINED COMMUNITIES (London: Haywood Gallery, 1995) p.4.

5 Norman Bryson, 'The Gaze in the Expanded Field', VISION AND VISUALITY, ed.Hal Foster (Seattle: Bay Press 1998) p.96.

6 Project proposal for further information see www.sti-project.net

7 Op. cit. Norman Bryson, pp.107–108.

8 Paul Virilio, 'Light Time', A LANDSCAPE OF EVENTS (Cambridge, Massachusetts: MIT Press, 2000) p.52.

Annabel Howland was born in 1967 in Bishop's Stortford, England and has lived in Amsterdam since 1992. From 1986–90 she studied at the Slade School of Fine Art, London and then graduated from the Jan van Eyck Akademie, Maastricht in 1992. She has exhibited in the Netherlands and internationally. Recent shows include NAVIGATION (Las Palmas, Rotterdam, 2001), ART STREAMS (Galerie Ron Mandos, Rotterdam, 2001), MULTIPEL MEERVOUD (De Parel, Amsterdam, 2001), HOTEL NEW YORK (PS1, New York,1999) and Mois de la Photo à Montréal (SKOL Centre des Arts Actuels, Montréal, 1999).

Annabel Howland

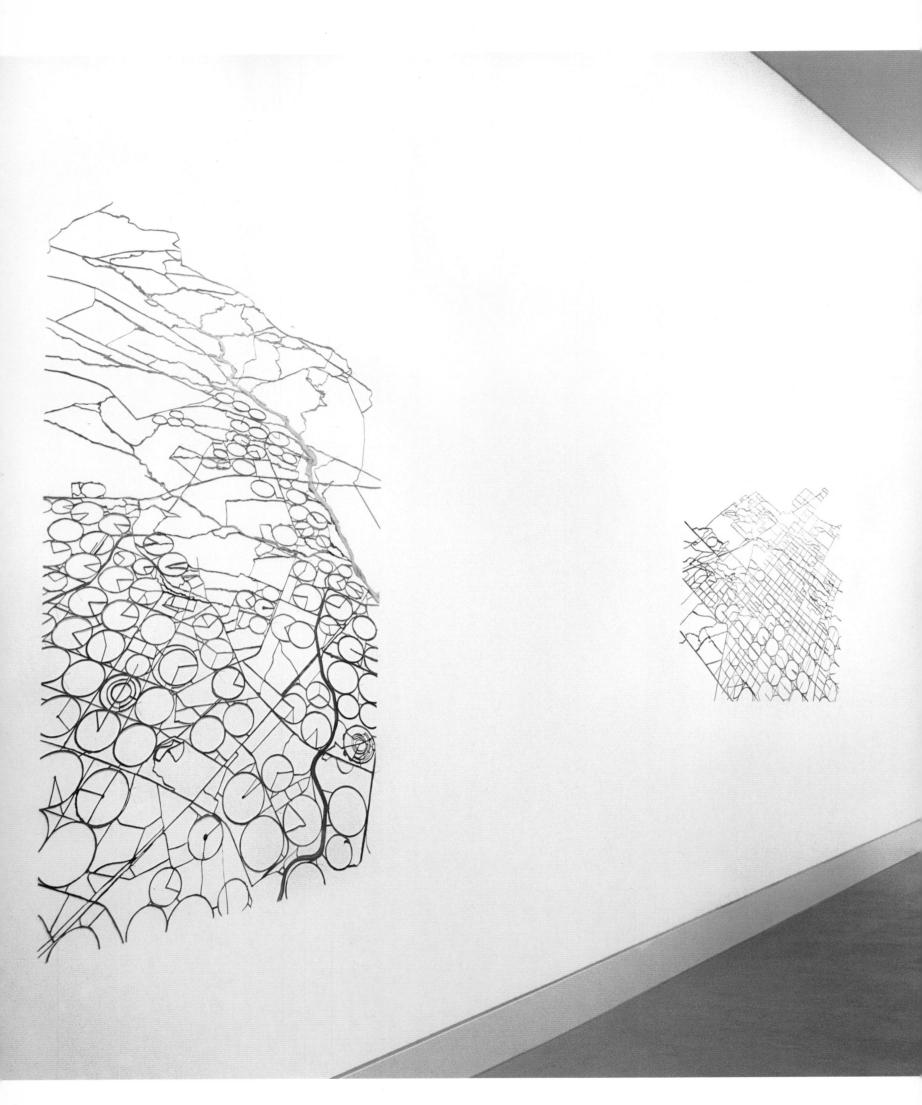

9

Cut Aerial I
2001
Lamda print
187 × 127 cm
RIGHT Detail

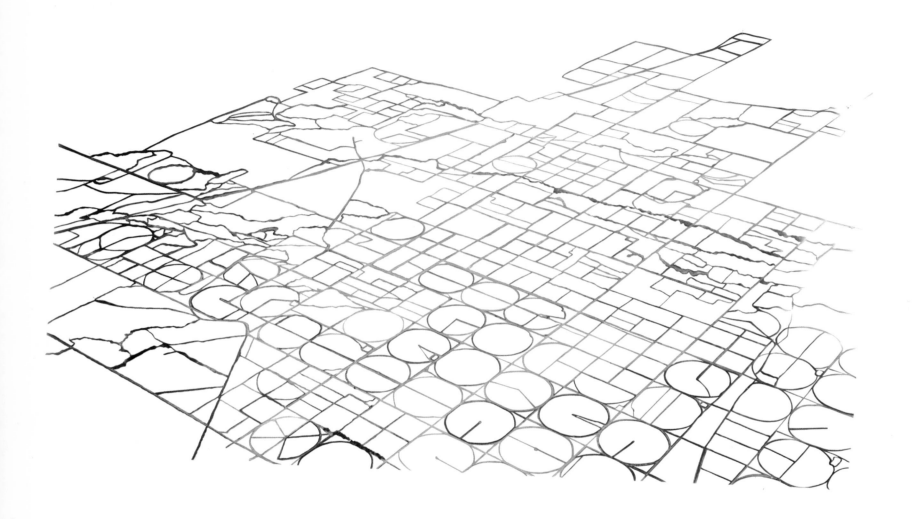

Cut Aerial II
2001
Lamda print
125 × 200 cm

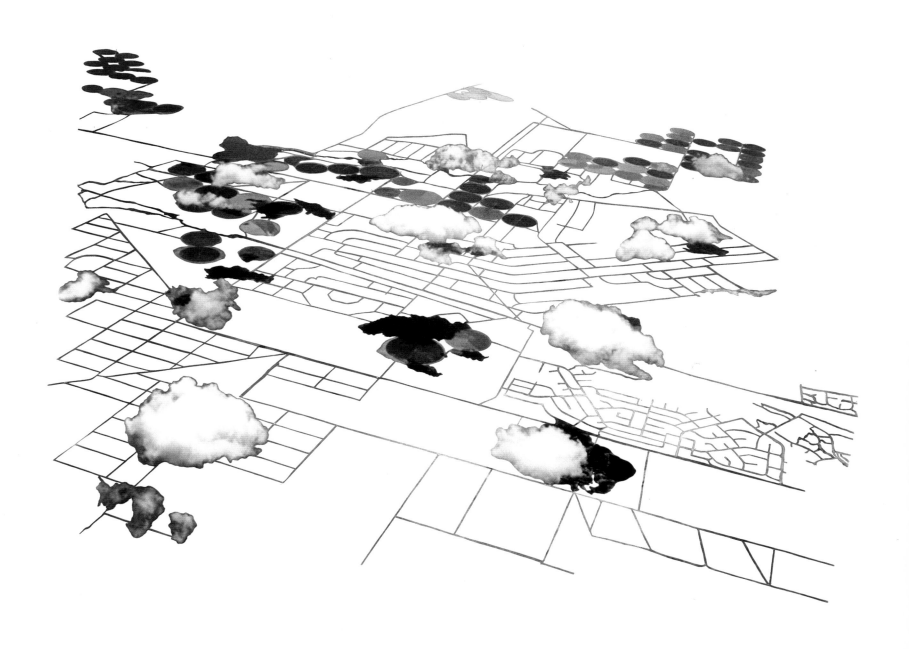

Cut Aerial III
2001
Lamda print
125 × 200 cm

Roadlines I
2000
Lamda print
70 × 245 cm

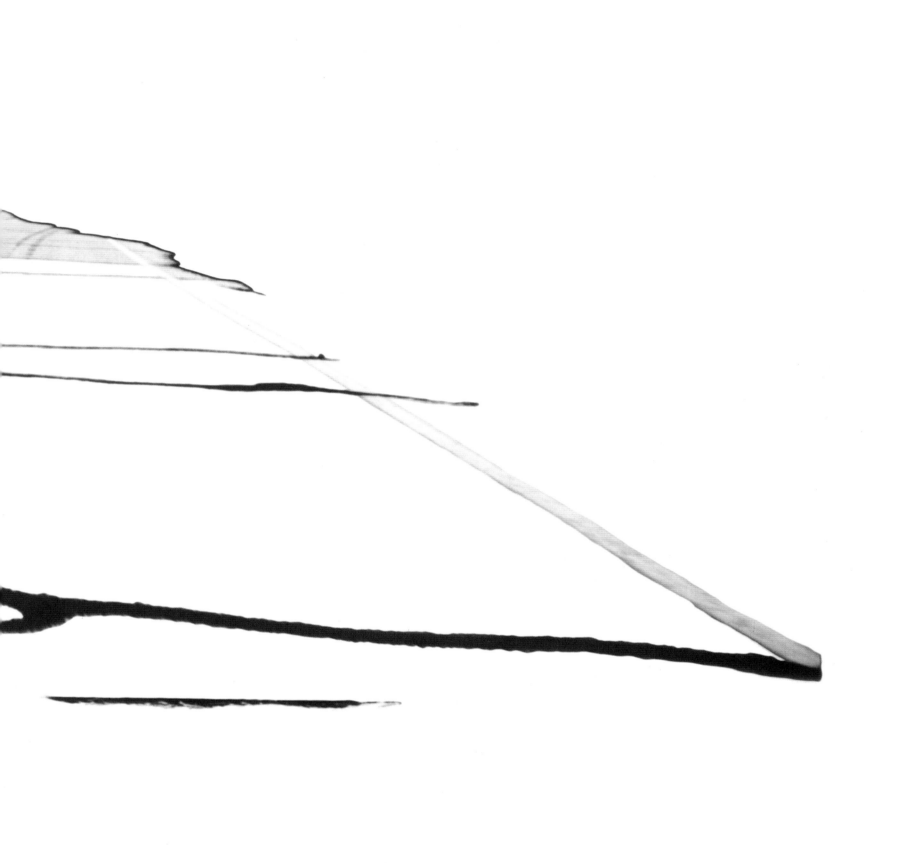

Henna Nadeem was born in 1966 in Leeds, England. She currently lives and works in London. She completed a BA in Fine Art at the John Moores University, Liverpool in 1989 and then graduated with an MA from the Royal College of Art, London in 1993. She has recently exhibited in RECORD COLLECTION (VTO Gallery, London, The International 3, Manchester and Forde Espace d'Art Contemporain, Geneva, 2001), RE:CREATION, RE:CONSTRUCTION (Pump House Gallery, London, 2001), THE POSTER SHOW (Cabinet Gallery, London, 2000), FABRICATIONS (Worcester City Art Gallery and Museum, 2000 and Norwich Gallery, 1999) and 000ZEROZEROZERO (Whitechapel Art Gallery, London, 1999).

Henna Nadeem

Black & White Cliffs
2001
Collage
41 × 46 cm

Orange Sunset
2001
Collage
37 × 46 cm

Big Black
2001
Collage
61 × 46 cm

Pale Green Trees
2001
Collage
57 × 39 cm

Joshua Trees
2001
Collage
22 × 64 cm

Orange Lake
2000
Collage
59 × 42 cm
RIGHT Detail

Ingrid Pollard was born in Georgetown, Guyana. She lives and works in London. She studied Film and Video at the London College of Printing and then, in 1995, graduated from the University of Derby with an MA in Photographic Studies. Recent exhibitions include HIDDEN HISTORIES, HIDDEN STORIES (University of Central Lancashire, Preston, 1999), STORY TIME/APPENDIX A (Jerusalem, Israel, 1998), TRANSFORMING THE CROWN (Caribbean Cultural Centre, New York, 1997) and BURSTING STONE (Beacon Gallery, Cumbria, 1997).

Ingrid Pollard

**Asymptotic – not falling
together**
2001
Digital print on vinyl
310 × 252 cm

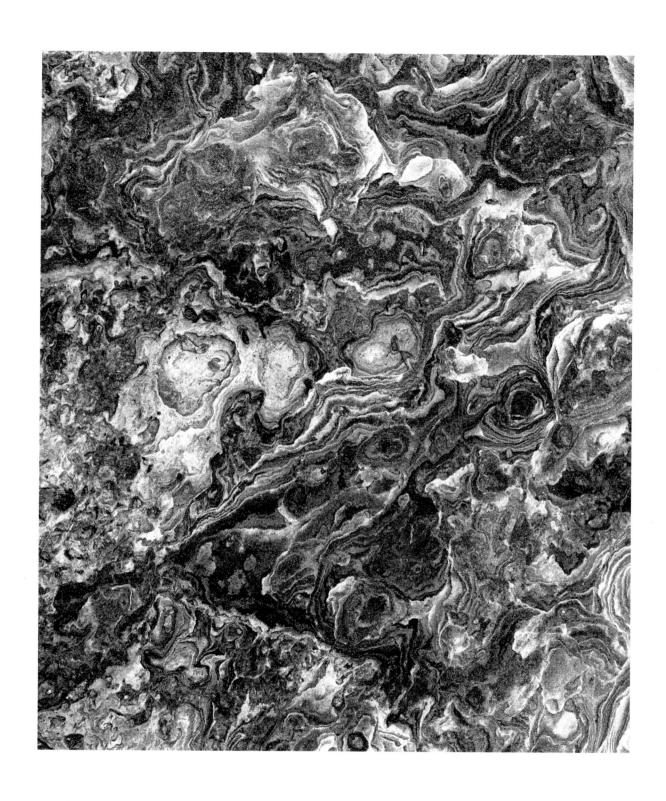

**Quondam – one that
once had, but no longer**
2001
Digital print on vinyl
310 × 252 cm
OVERLEAF Detail

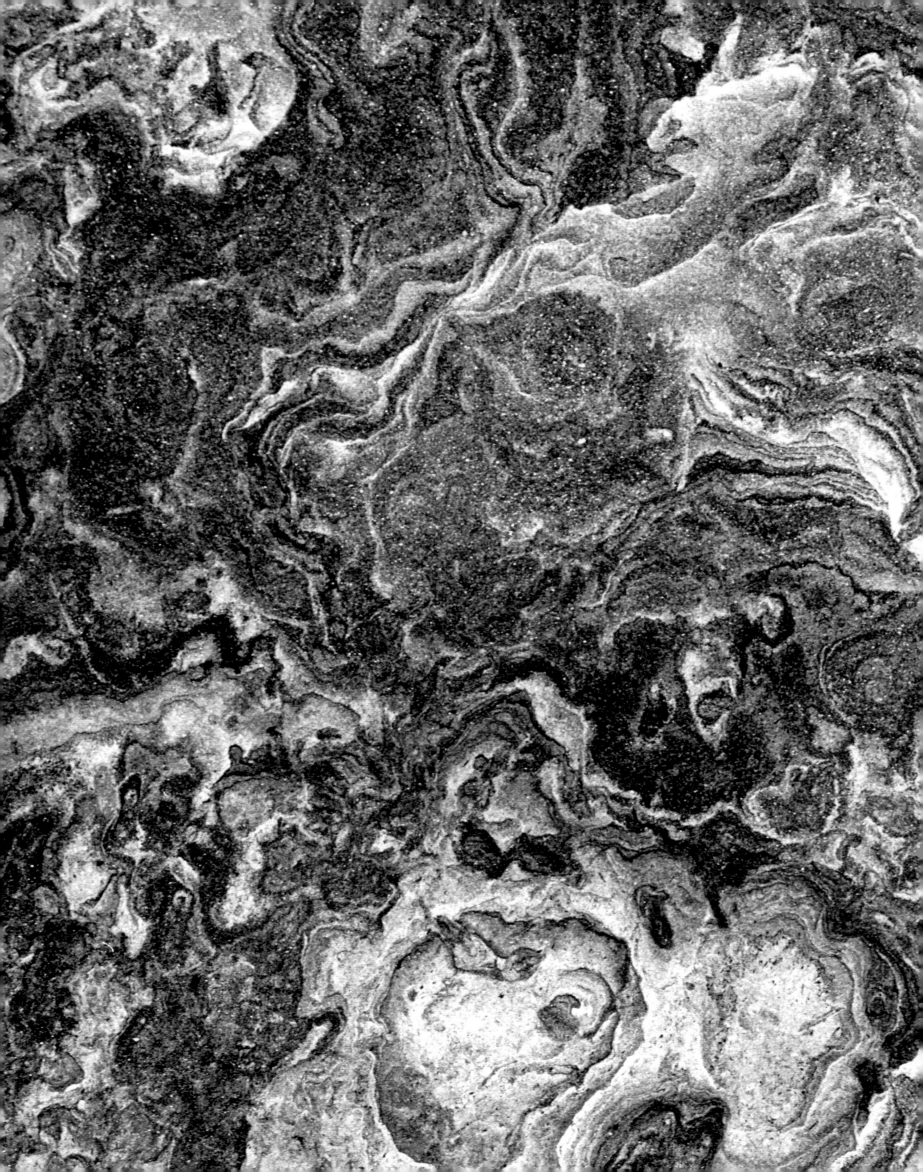

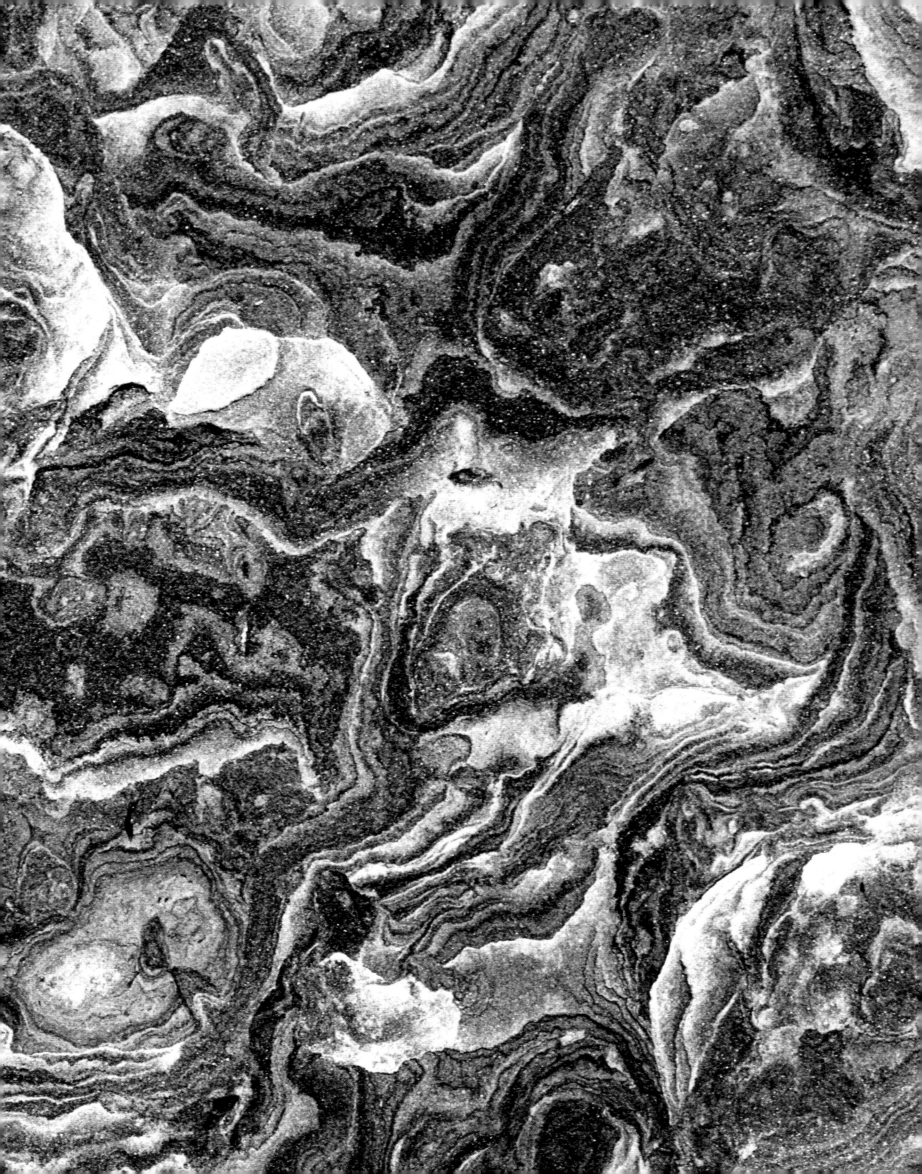

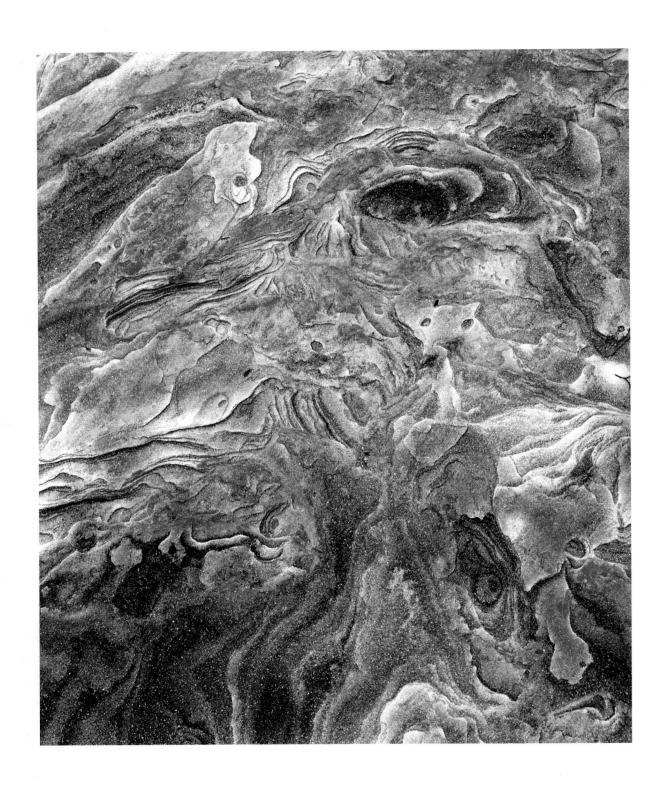

**Dehiscence – passing
through interstices of
membrane**
2001
Digital print on vinyl
310 × 252 cm

**Parabiosis – solid generated
by rotation**
2001
Digital print on vinyl
310 × 252 cm
OVERLEAF Detail

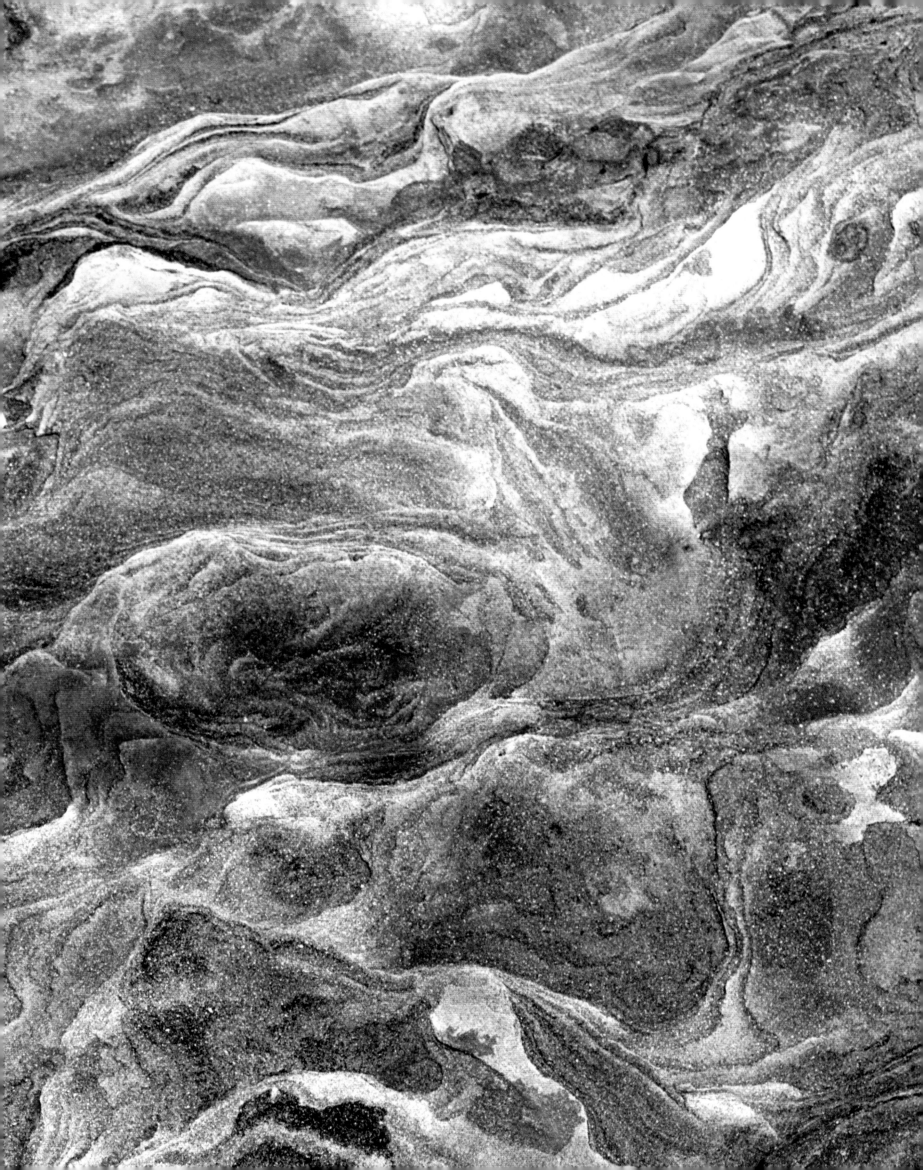

Camila Sposati was born in 1972 in São Paulo, Brazil and currently lives in Berlin. From 1991–96 she studied History at the University of São Paulo. She completed her Fine Art Postgraduate studies at Goldsmiths College in 2000. Recent exhibitions include UNCHAPERONED (Aroma Project Space, Berlin, 2001), PANDÆMONIUM (The Lux, London, 2001), EV+A – EXTENDED (Limerick, Ireland, 2001), ASSEMBLY (Stepney, London, 2000) and LIVING WITH THE DUTCH (House Project, London, 2000).

Camila Sposati

Talk to Me
2000
Stills from video installation
Pages 38–43

but the battery had run out
on my mobile.

what time did you try to call?

what a fucking

hangover

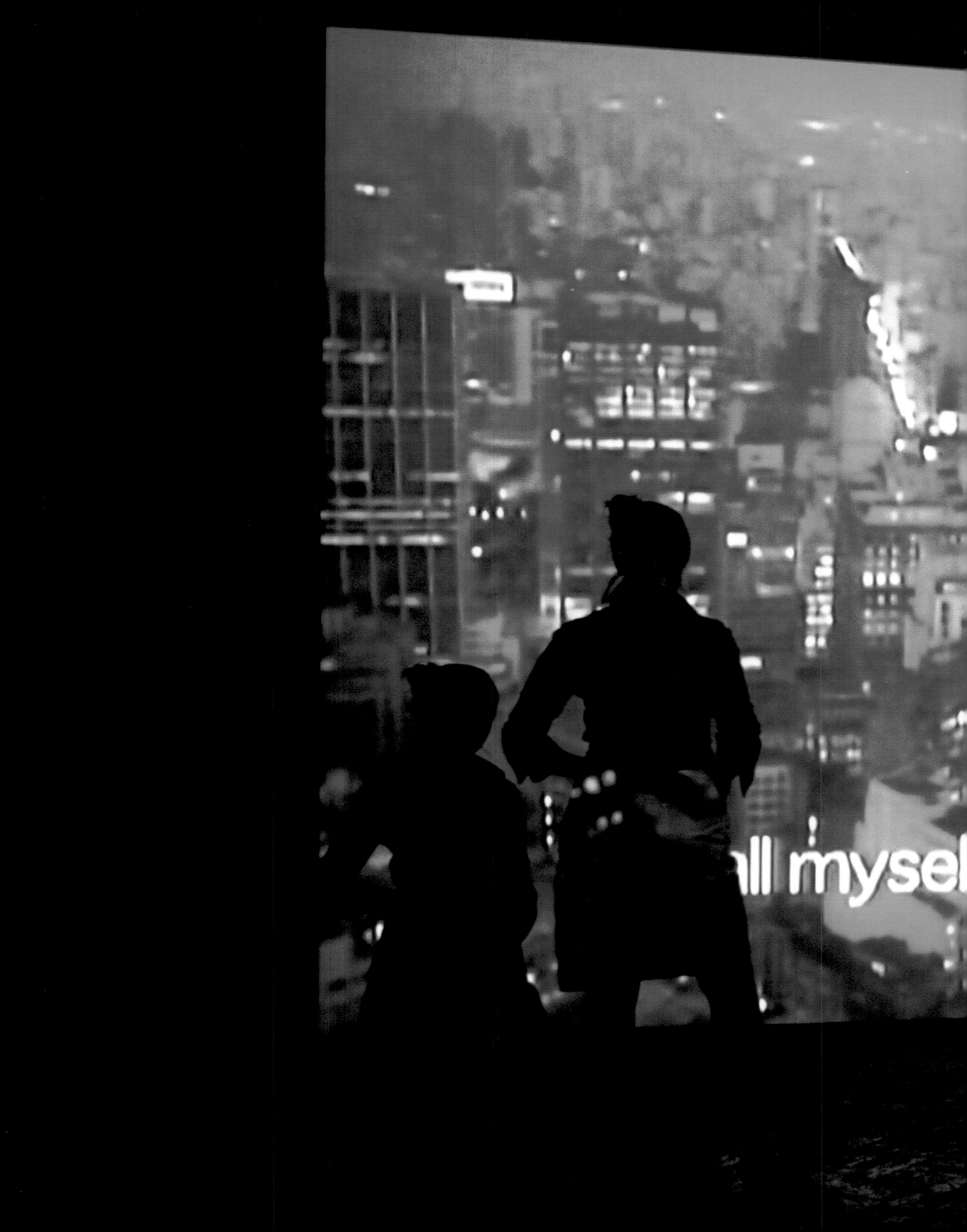
ll myse

Talk to Me
2000
Installation view
Dilston Grove

The Search for Terrestrial Intelligence (S.T.I. Consortium) brings together artists, scientists and technologists from a number disciplines and international research centres. MIKE PHILLIPS, GEOFF COX and CHRIS SPEED are researchers at the STAR Centre (Science, Technology and Art Research) at the Institute of Digital Art and Technology, University of Plymouth. ANGELO CANGELOSI and GUIDO BUGMANN are researchers in the field of Artificial Intelligence and Autonomous Robotics at the Centre for Neural and Adaptive Systems, also at the University of Plymouth. NICK VECK is the Technical Director at The National Remote Sensing Centre in Leicester and has worked in the Space Industry since 1977. CHRISTA SOMMERER and LAURENT MIGNONNEAU are currently working as artists and researchers at the ATR Media Integration and Communications Research Lab in Kyoto Japan. The S.T.I. system code has been developed in association with LIMBOMEDIA.COM and MEI CEN. The online version of the S.T.I. Consortium Project can be found at: www.sti-project.net

The Search for Terrestrial Intelligence (S.T.I. Consortium)

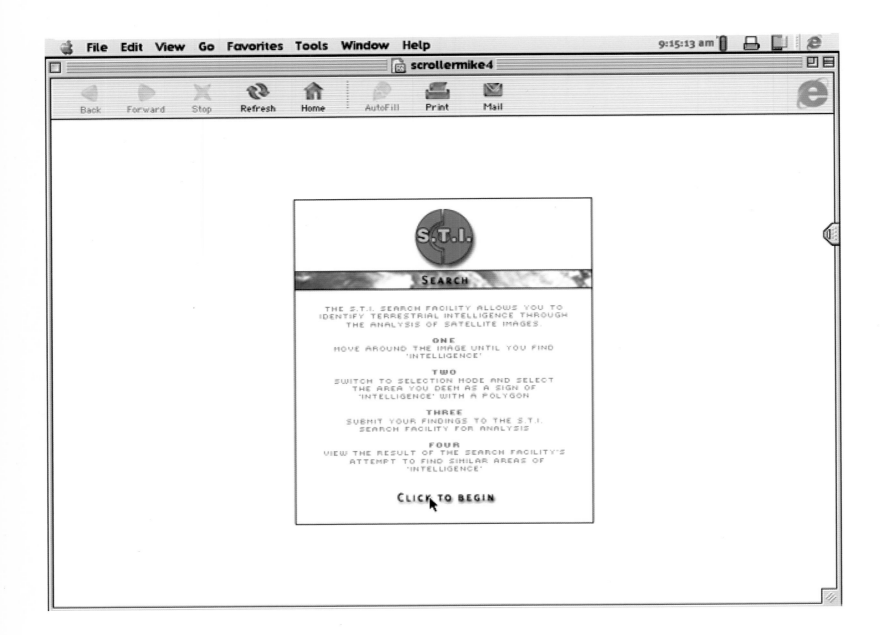

Click To Begin
2001
S.T.I. Search Engine
Shockwave front-end
to S.T.I. server

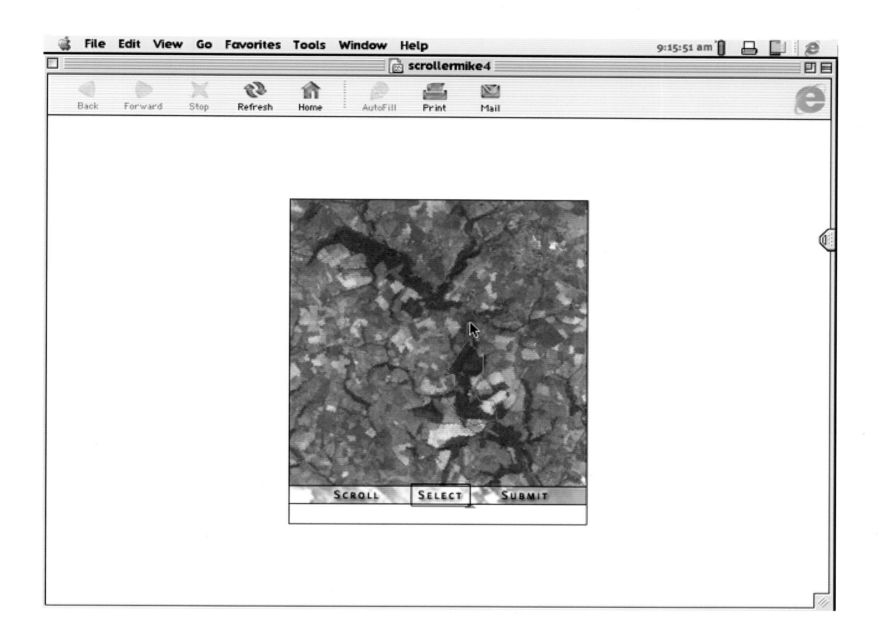

File Edit View Go Favorites Tools Window Help

9:15:51 am

Back   Forward   Stop   Refresh   Home   AutoFill   Print   Mail

SCROLL   SELECT   SUBMIT

Select
2001
Satellite image of earth
Lat 50° 26' Long 4° 18'
S.T.I. Search Engine
Shockwave front-end to
S.T.I. server

**S.T.I. Search Results/
Image Processor**
2001
factor in X: 13, factor in y:
13, mean red value of the
region: 217, mean green
value of the region: 185,
mean blue value of the
region: 139, variance red
value of the region: 16,
variance green value of the
region: 11, variance blue
value of the region: 11,
number of areas found . . .
Pages 50-51

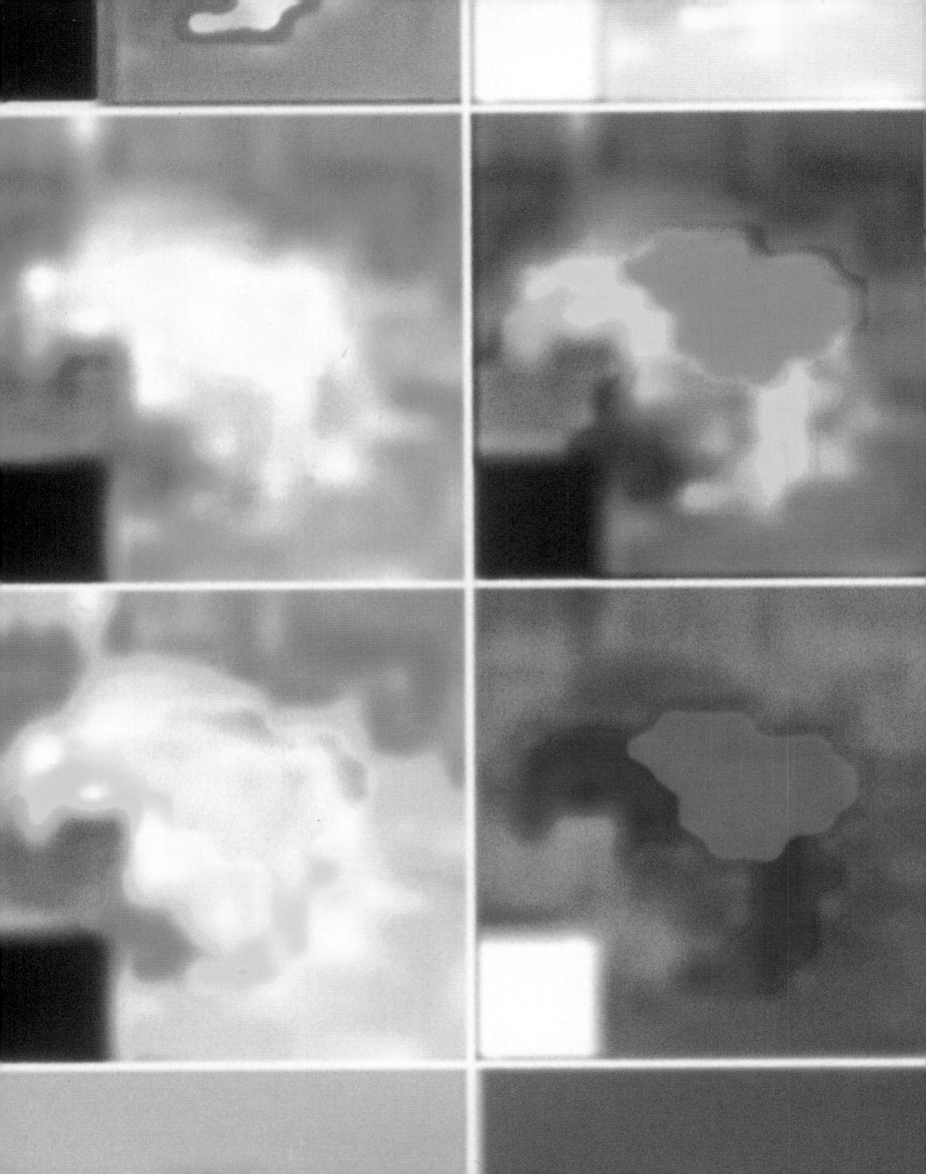

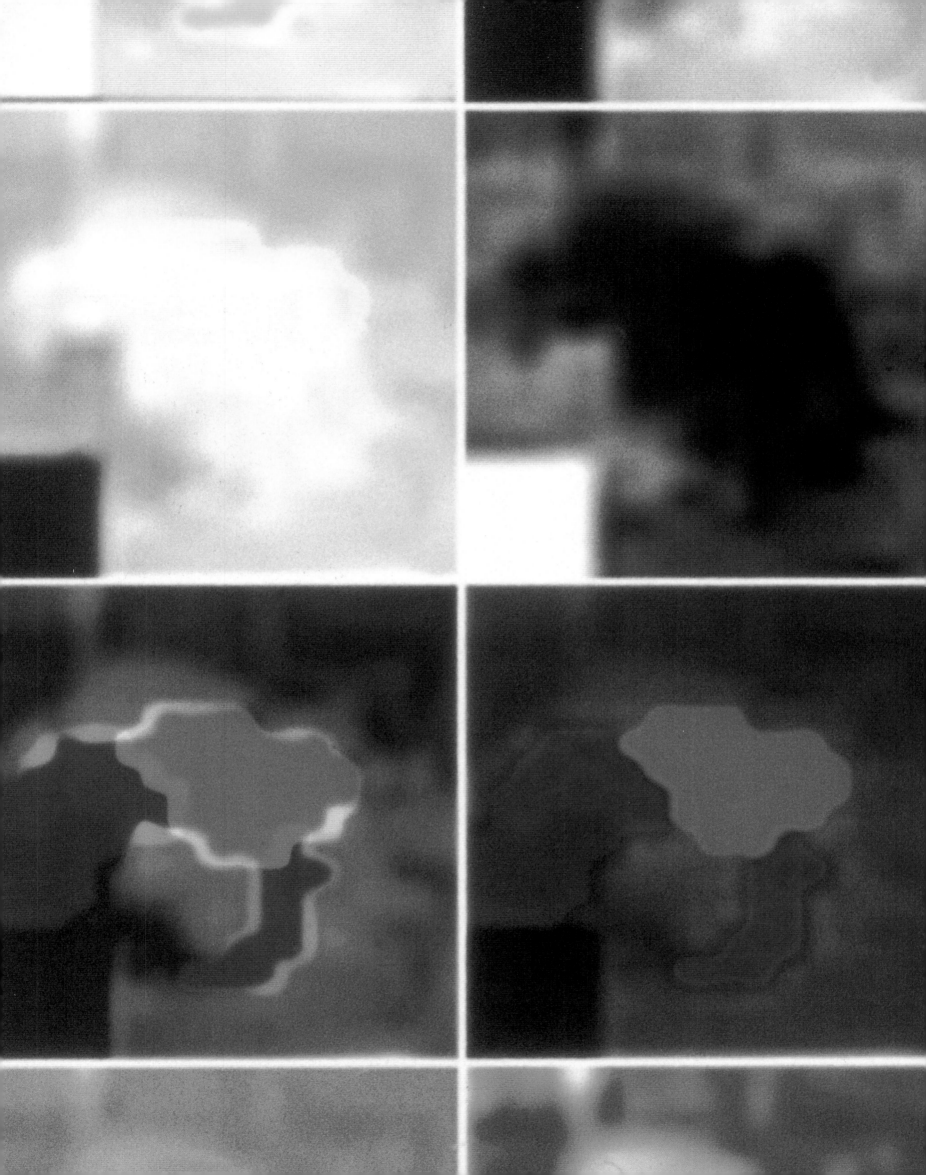

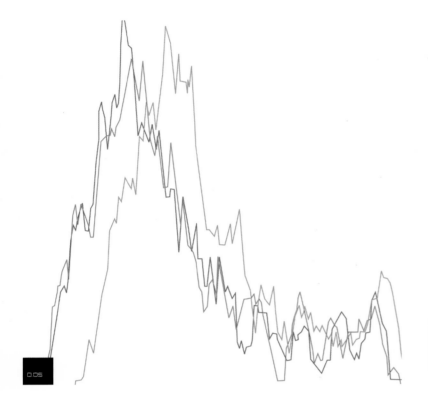

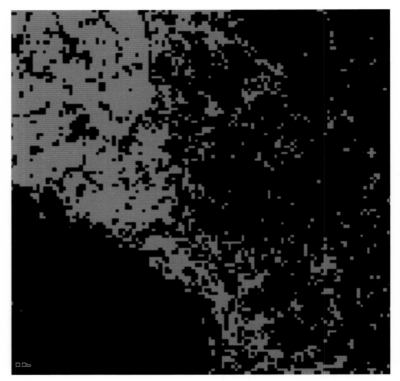

**S.T.I. Search Engine/
Image Processor**
2001
4 of 10 phases
0.05: frequency
histogram of pixel RGB
intensity values (0 to 255)
0.06-0.07: class search
for 5 × 5 pixel clusters
0.08: Bayesian statistical
analysis of pixel integrity

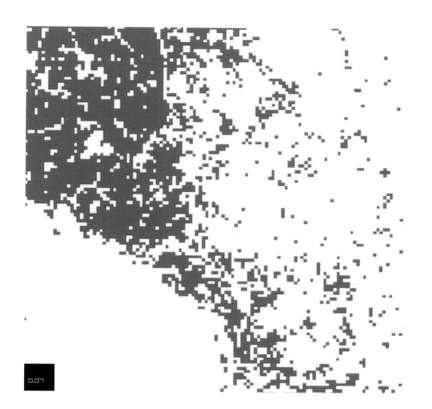

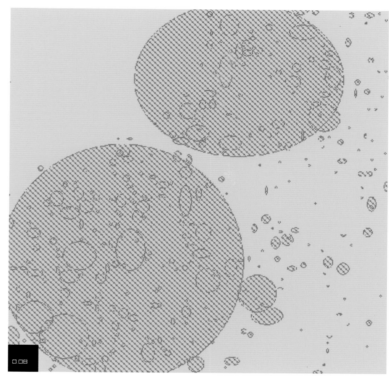

0,0),(0,0,0),(0,0,0),(0,0,0),(0,0,0),(0,0,0),(0,0,0),(0,0,0),(0,0,0),(0,0,0),(0,0,0),(0,0,0),(0,0,0),(0,0,0),(0,0,0
),(0,0,0),(0,0,0),(0,0,0),(0,0,0),(0,0,0),(0,0,0),(0,0,0),(0,0,0),(0,0,0),(0,0,0),(0,0,0),(0,0,0),(0,0,0),(0,0,0),
),(0,0,0),(0,0,0),(0,0,0),(0,0,0),(0,0,0),(0,0,0),(0,0,0),(0,0,0),(0,0,0),(0,0,0),(0,0,0),(0,0,0),(0,0,0),(0,0,0),(0
0,0,0),(0,0,0),(0,0,0),(0,0,0),(0,0,0),(0,0,0),(0,0,0),(0,0,0),(0,0,0),(0,0,0),(0,0,0),(0,0,0),(0,0,0),(0,0,0),(0,0
0,1),(0,0,1),(0,0,0),(0,0,0),(0,0,0),(0,0,0),(0,0,0),(0,0,0),(0,0,0),(0,0,0),(0,0,1),(0,0,1),(0,0,1
1),(1,0,1),(2,0,1),(1,0,0),(1,0,0),(1,0,0),(0,0,0),(1,0,0),(1,0,0),(1,0,0),(1,1,0),(1,1,0),(1,1,0),
),(0,0,0),(0,0,0),(0,0,0),(0,0,0),(0,0,1),(0,0,0),(0,0,0),(0,0,0),(0,0,0),(0,0,0),(0,0,0),(0,0,0),(0,0,0),(0
1,0,0),(0,0,0),(0,0,0),(0,0,0),(0,0,0),(0,0,0),(0,0,0),(0,0,0),(0,0,0),(0,0,0),(0,0,0),(0,0,0),(0,0,0),(0,0
0,0),(0,0,0),(0,0,1),(0,0,0),(0,0,0),(0,0,1),(0,1,1),(0,1,0),(0,1,1),(0,0,0),(0,1,0),(0,1,0),(0,1,0
1),(1,0,1),(1,1,1),(1,1,1),(1,1,1),(1,1,1),(1,1,0),(1,1,0),(1,1,0),(1,1,0),(1,0,0),(1,0,1),(1,0,0),
),(1,1,1),(1,1,1),(1,1,2),(1,2,2),(1,2,2),(1,2,2),(1,2,2),(1,2,2),(1,3,2),(1,4,2),(2,4,2),(2,3,1),(2,
3,1,0),(2,0,0),(2,0,0),(2,0,0),(1,0,0),(1,0,0),(1,0,0),(0,0,0),(0,0,0),(1,0,0),(0,0,0),$(275225,0
.343284,0.500000,0.246269,0.343284),(275225,0.343284,0.500000,0.246269,0.343284)
),(275225,0.343284,0.500000,0.246269,0.343284),(275225,0.343284,0.500000,0.246269,0
,0.343284),(275225,0.343284,0.500000,0.246269,0.343284),(275225,0.343284,0.500000,0
,0.246269,0.343284),(275225,0.343284,0.500000,0.246269,0.343284),(275225,0.343284,0
,0.500000,0.246269,0.343284),(275225,0.343284,0.500000,0.246269,0.343284),(275225,0
,0.343284,0.500000,0.246269,0.343284),(275225,0.343284,0.500000,0.246269,0.343284
4),(275225,0.343284,0.500000,0.246269,0.343284),(275225,0.343284,0.500000,0.246269
9,0.343284),(275225,0.343284,0.500000,0.246269,0.343284),(275225,0.343284,0.500000
0,0.246269,0.343284),(275225,0.343284,0.500000,0.246269,0.343284),(190280,0.164179
9,0.388060,0.253731,0.164179),(190280,0.164179,0.388060,0.253731,0.164179),(190280
0,0.164179,0.388060,0.253731,0.164179),(190280,0.164179,0.388060,0.253731,0.16417
79),(190280,0.164179,0.388060,0.253731,0.164179),(190280,0.164179,0.388060,0.25373
31,0.164179),(190280,0.164179,0.388060,0.253731,0.164179),(190280,0.164179,0.38806
60,0.253731,0.164179),(190280,0.164179,0.388060,0.253731,0.164179),(190280,0.16417
79,0.388060,0.253731,0.164179),(190280,0.164179,0.388060,0.253731,0.164179),(19028
80,0.164179,0.388060,0.253731,0.164179),(190280,0.164179,0.388060,0.253731,0.1641
79),(190280,0.164179,0.388060,0.253731,0.164179),(190280,0.164179,0.388060,0.2537
731,0.164179),(190280,0.164179,0.388060,0.253731,0.164179),(95520,0.223881,0.35820
9,0.156716,0.223881),(95520,0.223881,0.358209,0.156716,0.223881),(95520,0.223881,0
358209,0.156716,0.223881),(95520,0.223881,0.358209,0.156716,0.223881),(95520,0.223
3881,0.358209,0.156716,0.223881),(95520,0.223881,0.358209,0.156716,0.223881),(9552
0,0.223881,0.358209,0.156716,0.223881),(95520,0.223881,0.358209,0.156716,0.223881
),(95520,0.223881,0.358209,0.156716,0.223881),(95520,0.223881,0.358209,0.156716,0.2
23881),(95520,0.223881,0.358209,0.156716,0.223881),(95520,0.223881,0.358209,0.1567
16,0.223881),(95520,0.223881,0.358209,0.156716,0.223881),(95520,0.223881,0.358209
0.156716,0.223881),(95520,0.223881,0.358209,0.156716,0.223881),(95520,0.223881,0.35
8209,0.156716,0.223881),(100520,0.156716,0.358209,0.179104,0.156716),(100520,0.156
6716,0.358209,0.179104,0.156716),(100520,0.156716,0.358209,0.179104,0.156716),(10
00520,0.156716,0.358209,0.179104,0.156716),(100520,0.156716,0.358209,0.179104,0.15
56716),(100520,0.156716,0.358209,0.179104,0.156716),(100520,0.156716,0.358209,0.17
79104,0.156716),(100520,0.156716,0.358209,0.179104,0.156716),(100520,0.156716,0.3
58209,0.179104,0.156716),(100520,0.156716,0.358209,0.179104,0.156716),(100520,0.15
56716,0.358209,0.179104,0.156716),(100520,0.156716,0.358209,0.179104,0.156716),(1
100520,0.156716,0.358209,0.179104,0.156716),(100520,0.156716,0.358209,0.179104,0.
156716),(100520,0.156716,0.358209,0.179104,0.156716),(100520,0.156716,0.358209,0.
179104,0.156716),(95525,0.276119,0.358209,0.171642,0.276119),(95525,0.276119,0.35
8209,0.171642,0.276119),(95525,0.276119,0.358209,0.171642,0.276119),(95525,0.27611
9,0.358209,0.171642,0.276119),(95525,0.276119,0.358209,0.171642,0.276119),(95525,0
276119,0.358209,0.171642,0.276119),(95525,0.276119,0.358209,0.171642,0.276119),(9
5525,0.276119,0.358209,0.171642,0.276119),(95525,0.276119,0.358209,0.171642,0.276
19),(95525,0.276119,0.358209,0.171642,0.276119),(95525,0.276119,0.358209,0.171642
0.276119),(95525,0.276119,0.358209,0.171642,0.276119),(95525,0.276119,0.358209,0.1
1642,0.276119),(95525,0.276119,0.358209,0.171642,0.276119),(95525,0.276119,0.3582
09,0.171642,0.276119),(95525,0.276119,0.358209,0.171642,0.276119),(95525,0.276119,0
0.335821,0.179104,0.171642),(100540,0.171642,0.335821,0.179104,0.171642),(100540,0
0.171642,0.335821,0.179104,0.171642),(100540,0.171642,0.335821,0.179104,0.171642
),(100540,0.171642,0.335821,0.179104,0.171642),(100540,0.171642,0.335821,0.179104
,0.171642),(100540,0.171642,0.335821,0.179104,0.171642),(100540,0.171642,0.335821
,0.179104,0.171642),(100540,0.171642,0.335821,0.179104,0.171642),(100540,0.171642
,0.335821,0.179104,0.171642),(100540,0.171642,0.335821,0.179104,0.171642),(100540
,0.171642,0.335821,0.179104,0.171642),(100540,0.171642,0.335821,0.179104,0.171642

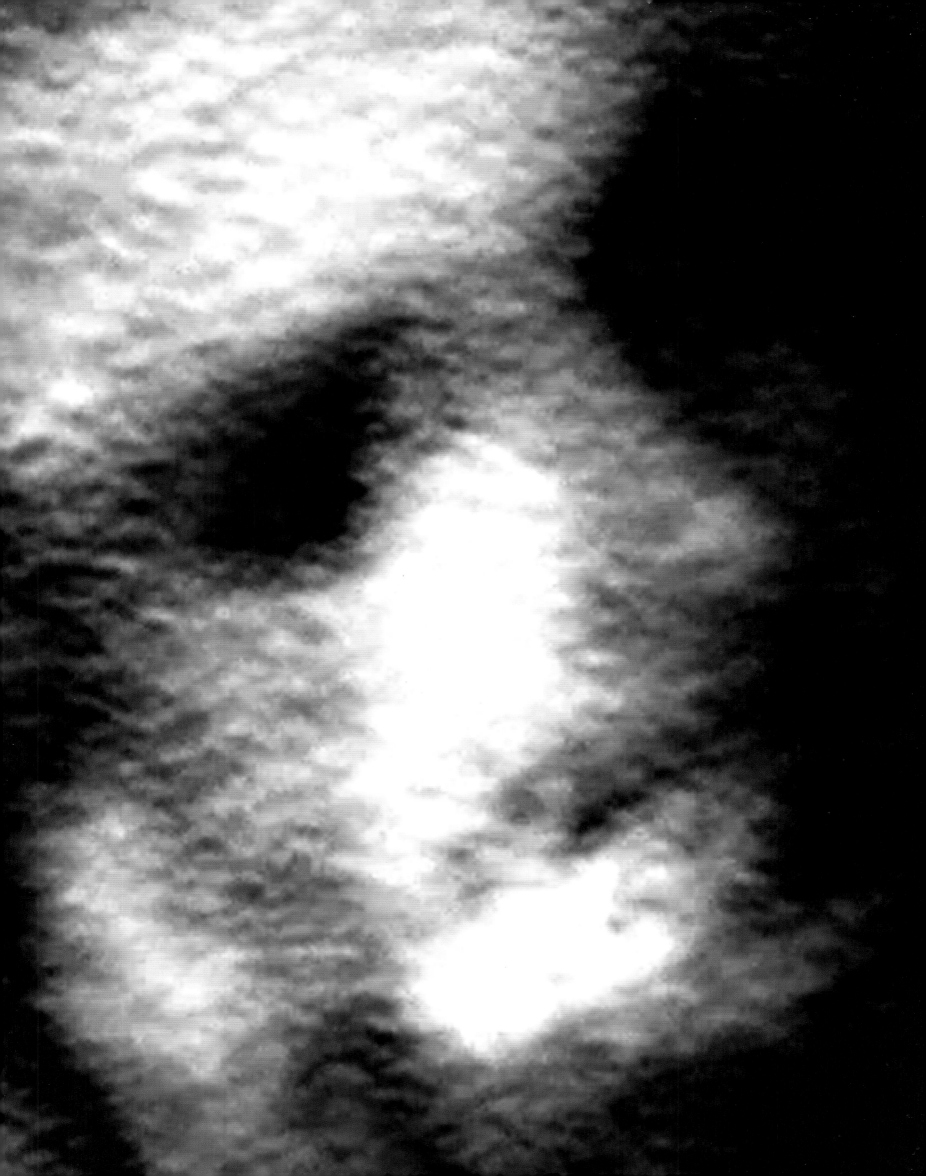

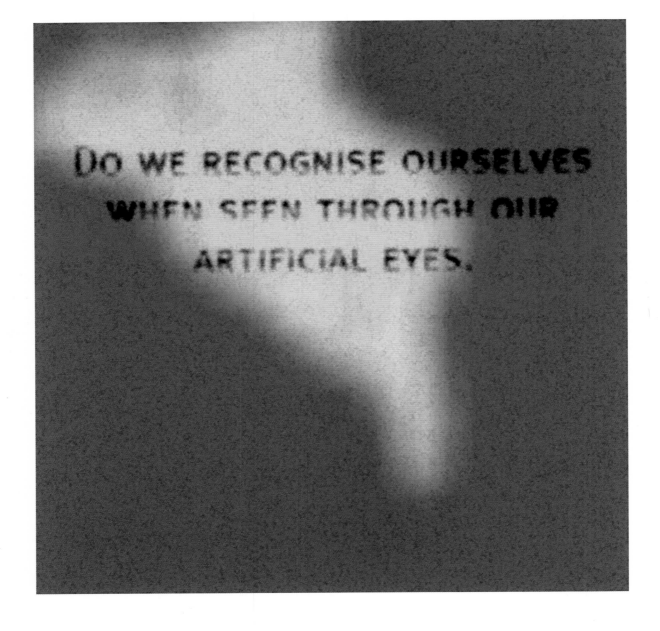

S.T.I. Narcissus Movie [v1.0]
2001
Frame # 00:06:03
Digital video

Jorella Andrews

Dispossessing the land

I

Contemporary discussions of landscape generally evoke notions of crisis. In a recent essay published in ARTNEWS, the critic Hilarie M. Sheets refers to "our precarious contemporary moment, when technology and modern habits have so altered the landscape".[1] The online documentation for this exhibition asks a related question. "At this point in time, does the term landscape merely conjure up idyllic notions of the countryside? Or, is the seemingly never-ending industrial malaise in the countryside symptomatic of a broader crisis of identity which has begun to erode the distinctions between the metropolitan and the rural tradition?"[2] However, the sense of trauma implicit in the landscape-oriented works at issue here is also of another order.

Clearly, landscape is culture: nature that has been handled, and mishandled. Originally a term in painting, landscape (sixteenth century: LANDSKIP) is, more specifically, the land viewed, imagined, conceptualized and depicted from particular (and largely culturally-inflected) perspectives. It is the land plus us. Or, more evocatively, it is the land as it exists in and through us: "The landscape thinks itself in me and I am its consciousness", Cézanne is reputed to have said, as he looked and painted.[3] It is also that through which (or in relation to which) we think ourselves. The words 'landscape trauma', then, suggest discontinuities, disruptions to those interrelationships, to those ways of perceiving, imagining, conceptualizing and representing the world, self and others.

The recent works of Annabel Howland, Henna Nadeem, Ingrid Pollard, Camila Sposati and the STI Consortium explore these varied entanglements and orientations, and also provoke their disruption. These interventions are all the more interesting since the technologies of representation at issue in each case are connected with the photographic – a medium that at first appearance disavows the realities of lived entanglement between viewer and viewed. Indeed, it still largely figures in the contemporary cultural imagination as that which not only extends human perception, but rarefies it, making it objective, impassive and dissociated. As Susan Sontag has put it in her essay 'In Plato's Cave': "What is written about a person or an event [or indeed a place] is frankly an interpretation, as are handmade visual statements, like paintings and drawings. Photographed images do not seem to be statements about the world so much as pieces of it, miniatures of reality . . . ."[4] And again, "Photographing is essentially an act of non-intervention . . . . To take a picture is to have an interest in things as they are, in the status

1 Hilarie M. Sheets, 'Reinventing the Landscape', ARTNEWS (March 2001) pp. 128–133.

2 http://www. autograph-abp.co.uk/ archive/whatson.html

3 Cited in Maurice Merleau-Ponty, 'Cézanne's Doubt', SENSE AND NON-SENSE (Evanston: Northwestern University Press, 1964) p. 17.

4 Susan Sontag, 'In Plato's Cave', ON PHOTOGRAPHY (Harmondsworth: Penguin Books, 1977) p. 4.

5 Ibid., pp. 11, 12.

6 Ibid., p. 7.

7 Ibid., p. 4.

quo remaining unchanged (at least as long as it takes to get a 'good' picture) . . . ." [5] As far as these works are concerned, such definitions are found to be without substance. For in challenging the ways in which we perceive and conceive of the environments that surround (and arguably also define) us, they inevitably also unsettle our usual ways of looking at, and thinking about, the photographic. For instance, the aggression that Sontag claims is implicit "in every use of the camera" [6] is not, in these works, primarily directed at that which is being 'shot' or 'captured' photographically. Rather, a kind of (productive) aggression is meted out upon the photographic process itself, and/or upon its products. Significantly though (and this is a second area of agreement amongst all the works here), this aggression has produced images that are immensely satisfying on an aesthetic level. They are all, in their different ways, undeniably beautiful. What these works also open up then are notions of the aesthetic, and specifically the beautiful, as a potent critical tool.

Another point is also worth making here, since it again relates to the subversion of interpretative norms associated with the medium of photography. Sontag (if I may quote her yet again) writes that to photograph "is to appropriate the thing photographed. It means putting oneself into a certain relation to the world that feels like knowledge – and, therefore, like power." [7] This position of authority is generally seen not only to relate, as here, to the USE of the photographic, but also to a particular kind of perspective on things for which photography is arguably well suited: the so-called 'view from above'. A further representational strategy that is shared by these artists is their evocation, albeit in different ways and to differing degrees, of precisely this viewing position. But here it provides neither certainty and clarity on the one hand, nor a sense of human distance, non-involvement and disinterestedness, on the other.

All these works raise questions about the nature of location and locatedness. In Camila Sposati's video TALK TO ME (2000), aerial views of a city (São Paulo) seem both to recall and undermine a filmic convention: that of the establishing shot. For ironically, no clear sense of place or context is ever provided. Although cuts in the visual sequence indicate the passing of time (the gradual transition from dull day to glittering night), spatially we are left to drift above anonymous urban gridlines, and through an ever-unfolding but never-ending image without edges. The film's soundtrack inserts into this another spatiality and temporality. For the three minutes of the video's duration, we are thrown into a real-time fragment of strangely disconnected conversation between a man and woman, so disjointed that it is unclear, at first, that they are talking to each other. Their voices resonate with a sense of interior space (presumably they are 'down there' and inside, somewhere), but they don't seem to hear or see each other. It is as if halves of two separate telephone conversations have, for no apparent reason, become spliced. Only at the end does it become apparent that they are, indeed, together. Gradually, as the video loops back to the beginning, and is watched again and again, a sense of the conversation's unique choreography begins to emerge. (Unresolved) connections and a kind of intimacy form among its unanswered questions, mundane observations, reveries and reports.

The video questions locatedness and initiates processes of decipherment in two further ways. First, due to the uncertain manner in which the visuals relate to the soundtrack, it is unclear how the urban scene should be read. Does it function as a backdrop to the conversation, or, given the temporal disjunctions at issue, is it somehow illustrative of what is being said (and not said)? Or is it a partly imagined scene, PRODUCED by their words and their silences? For as the conversation shifts, the nature of the cityscape seems to shift as well, from patterned surface to human habitation, from generator of fantasies to no-place, to "this fucking place". Second, there is Sposati's camera work. The views given to us seem to have been produced by a drifting rather than a purposefully directed camera, a camera at once tethered to the city below, and floating above it, on wind and weather. On the one hand, its 'looking' is from afar. But its movements are also intimate and vulnerable, echoing the vagaries of the physical, psychological and emotional locatedness of the speakers.

Extreme alterations in scale and apparent viewing position are also generated by Ingrid Pollard's large photographic works – depictions of geological micro-formations which take on the appearance of complex tracts of land as they might be charted by aerial photography or cartographic means. But these works do not only shift us from the very large to the very small and back again. On the one hand, through entirely non-figurative means, they also plunge us into fantastical, haunted worlds, abstract yet surreal. The texture of digital print on vinyl produces an eerie glitter and a surface one cannot believe is flat (or will remain flat). And so, on the other hand, these works have uncanny power suddenly to shift our attention from mind to body. For somehow, these swirling, printed surfaces conjure up,

8 Merleau-Ponty also makes this point elsewhere: "Inevitably the roles between him [the painter] and the visible are reversed. That is why so many painters have said that things look at them. As André Marchand says, after Klee: 'In a forest, I have felt many times over that it was not I who looked at the forest. Some days I felt that the trees were looking at me . . . .'" 'Eye and Mind', THE PRIMACY OF PERCEPTION (Evanston: Northwestern University Press, 1964), p. 167.

9 Maurice Merleau-Ponty, THE VISIBLE AND THE INVISIBLE (Evanston: Northwestern University Press, 1964) p. 139.

10 Ovid, METAMORPHOSIS, trans. A. D. Melville (Oxford and New York: Oxford University Press, 1986) pp. 63, 64.

11 Ibid., p. 66.

and resonate with, the human body. Specifically, they speak to, and of, the surfaces of bodies, perhaps one's own, of skin stretched out, flayed, forced to accommodate an unfamiliar rectilinear frame. The titles of these works are evocative of such transmutations: ASYMPTOTIC – NOT FALLING TOGETHER; PARABIOSIS – SOLID GENERATED BY ROTATION; QUONDAM – ONE THAT ONCE HAD, BUT NO LONGER and DEHISCENCE – PASSING THROUGH INTERSTICES OF MEMBRANE (all 2001). The latter, with its reference to 'dehiscence', recalls the writing of French philosopher Maurice Merleau-Ponty. In his late work, THE VISIBLE AND THE INVISIBLE, he describes what he understands to be the particular dimensionality of the lived, perceiving body and the relationship of promiscuity/haunting between seers and that which they see. His words are worth repeating here.

> Thus since the seer is caught up in what he sees, it is still himself he sees: there is a fundamental narcissism of all vision. And thus, for the same reason, the vision he exercises, he also undergoes from the things, such that, as many painters have said, I feel myself looked at by the things,[8] my activity is equally passivity – which is the second and more profound sense of the narcissism: not to see in the outside, as the others see it, the contour of a body one inhabits, but especially to be seen by the outside, to exist within it, to EMIGRATE INTO IT, TO BE SEDUCED, CAPTIVATED, ALIENATED BY THE PHANTOM, SO THAT THE SEER AND THE VISIBLE RECIPROCATE ONE ANOTHER AND WE NO LONGER KNOW WHICH SEES AND WHICH IS SEEN. [Emphasis mine][9]

The pattern of perception described here as narcissistic (and which is also evoked by Pollard's works) has a doubled aspect. On the one hand, it involves actively seeing oneself, being "open to oneself" or "destined to oneself". But on the other hand, it also means being on the receiving end of vision and thus estranged from oneself. We are "seduced, captivated, [and] alienated by the phantom". As in Ovid's myth, narcissism involves both recognition and mis-recognition: "Himself he longs for, longs unwittingly . . . . Not knowing what he sees, he adores the sight . . . ."[10] The seer sees himself from the outside as "other", is filled with longing, and plunges into that which he can never finally grasp. Ultimately, however, this is a transformative act. Narcissus dies to one mode of being and is reborn into another:

> . . . but no body anywhere; /And in its stead they found a flower – behold, /White petals clustered round a cup of gold![11]

The unstable dynamics of connectedness and defamiliarization, of recognition and misrecognition, are also central to NARCISSUS V.1.0., the online project created by The Search for Terrestrial Intelligence, a consortium of artists, scientists and technologists working in research centres in Britain and Japan. Making use of powerful satellite imaging systems used in the exploration of outer space, they turn instead to an investigation of our own planet and of ourselves. But what these autonomous, remote sensing systems deliver is opacity and, from their positions of radical SURveillance, a kind of DISpossession of the earth. Our world emerges as odd, a network of indecipherable sounds and sights, signs, ideograms. In fact, as indicated by the project's title, it is unclear to what degree the technology in question discovers and documents these phenomena, or is itself the generator of them, merely imaging itself and its own processes. This is an old question, and a point of connection between the mechanical seeing at issue here, and our own human seeing. Web pages of flickering text pose other, related questions. What of our increasing reliance upon technologies that do our seeing for us? Will these autonomous systems 'know' the truth when they see it? Do we recognise ourselves when we see through our artificial eyes? And a question evoked by my own looking: is there a technological imaginary, just as there is a human one? And what might be their interrelationship? However, what at first appears as a thwarted quest for illumination, and a trail of misdirection, alters when confused attempts at decipherment are abandoned and the aesthetic sense kicks in. For then a multiplicity of complex structures, patterns and rhythms become apparent, testifying to and resonating with another (more bodily) order of intelligence.

In the works of Annabel Howland and Henna Nadeem the theme of (potentially productive) dispossession emerges once again. In the exhibition documentation, Howland's large photographic landscapes are described as having been "cut away nearly to the point of dissipation" and as "teetering on the edge of coherence and collapse." [12] ROADLINES I and II (2000) are ink-jet images mounted on foamex and then cut away to create sparse calligraphic gestures, fragile but nonetheless emphatic. Her later pieces, Cut AERIAL I, II and III (2001), are more complex and delicate. The landscape is again emptied of its content and made schematic, a network of signs which vary in their legibility (to what, for instance, do the circular forms repeated in CUT AERIAL I refer?). In addition, these works have been left unmounted, no more than fragile paper webs, lightly pinned to the wall. They would fold away to almost nothing in your hand. As the receding, perspectively rendered gridlines (indicating roads, fields, industrial estates?) waver towards disappearance,

12 Exhibition handout: LANDSCAPE TRAUMA IN THE AGE OF SCOPOPHILIA, thegallery and Dilston Grove (both Southwark Park), 4 July–5 August 2001.

13 Diana Yeh, 'Picnic Papers: The Botanical Surgeries of Henna Nadeem', MAKE 85 (September – November 1999) p. 30.

the horizontal slams into verticality, and the works pulsate instead with pattern.

Cutting is also central to the construction of Henna Nadeem's works, but they challenge our perception through processes of addition rather than subtraction. Her collages of appropriated landscape photographs from books and magazines convey a thickness of presence. But they also have the power to dispossess. This occurs through the juxtaposition of two different idealisations of land- and seascape. There are the seductive rural scenes (artificial worlds of touristic possession) which comprise the backgrounds to these pieces. And there are those images that overlie them – scenes that have been "carved into stylised patterns of geometric formations", some reminiscent of the designs of William Morris, others of Islamic motifs.[13] The nature of these juxtapositions alter from work to work. In BOUND and CALIFORNIA (both 1999) two different images have been brought together. In ORANGE LAKE and SUMMIT (both 2000), the same images have been used for fore- and background, but with their alignment displaced, making the distinctions between layers difficult to ascertain in places. We find ourselves mildly (but thus all the more intriguingly) disoriented as our attention slowly shifts between scene and pattern, and as two orders of looking are coupled. Pertinent is the fact that unease has been produced precisely through the use of the decorative; the patterned screens or veils function both as frames and as barriers, keeping us at a distance.

II

"The less I seek my source for some definitive
The closer I am to fine."
Indigo Girls, CLOSER TO FINE (Words: E. Saliers)

The works of Nadeem, Howland, the STI Consortium, Pollard and Sposati were curated by Richard Hylton for Autograph, the Association of Black Photographers in the UK. This fact does not compel me to bring questions of identity and identity politics into play, but it seems appropriate to do so. Why? Because, the way in which we perceive, imagine, conceptualize and represent the land to ourselves has everything to do with such matters. Religious intolerance is generally cited as a prime motivator of human conflict. But perhaps an even more fundamental, and often interconnected, root cause is our insistence that notions of personal and collective identity be tied to the exclusive possession of this or that particular tract of land. In the early stages of writing this essay I visited the exhibition MIGRATIONS: HUMANITY IN TRANSITION. Here, photographs by Sebastião Salgado documented the plight (and fortitude) of people the world over, who have been exiled or dispossessed because they have become embroiled (as victims and/or perpetrators) in precisely such divisiveness.[14] I write, now, in the aftermath of the terrorist attacks of 11 September 2001 upon New York City and Washington D.C., actions which are again a possible consequence of on-going conflict over the purportedly rightful possession of land.

We need to think of ourselves, and others, differently. Why cannot identity be linked instead to productive modes of orientation towards others, such as the generous stewardship and sharing of the earth and its resources? But such an alteration, if it were really to be lived out, would need to occur not only on the relatively fickle level of reason. It would need to be incorporated into our deepest levels of physical, emotional, spiritual and imaginative being. I believe that works such as these can help. Not through exhortation or by expounding upon specifics, but by initiating us into the fearful pleasures and pleasurable fears of seeing and being otherwise. Through formal, non-representational and aesthetic means, and perhaps only for a brief moment, these works bring us into openness and into the particular, creative uncertainties that are associated with freely made acts of dispossession. Their strategies of disruption are vital. For it would seem that this kind of openness can be achieved only by passing through and making use of those instances of traumatic dislocation with which we may from time to time be confronted. John Lechte reflects upon this idea as it is found in the writings of theorist and psychoanalyst Julia Kristeva:

> Trauma, crisis and perturbation . . . should be seen as the sources of an 'event' in the life of a subject, something which broadens horizons, and not something to be denied or resisted with a resultant atrophying of psychic space. To the extent that the crisis is absorbed into the psychical structure, the latter becomes increasingly more complex and supple, increasingly more capable of love.[15]

14 Sebastião Salgado, MIGRATIONS: HUMANITY IN TRANSITION, City Art Centre, Edinburgh, 30 June–2 September 2001.

15 John Lechte, 'Art, Love and Melancholy in the Work of Julia Kristeva' in ABJECTION, MELANCHOLIA AND LOVE: THE WORK OF JULIA KRISTEVA, eds. John Fletcher and Andrew Benjamin (London and New York: Routledge, 1990) pp. 32–33.

Jorella Andrews is a lecturer in Art History at Goldsmiths College, University of London. She is also on the editorial board of the art journal THIRD TEXT.

Acknowledgements

The production of a touring show can at times be a most arduous task, particularly in terms of securing venues. For this reason I am particularly grateful to Ron Henocq from thegallery (formerly Cafe Gallery) and Moira Innes from Leeds Metropolitan University Gallery for their support and commitment to hosting LANDSCAPE TRAUMA.

The opportunity to commission new works and a publication for the exhibition has been made possible by generous financial support received from the National Touring Lottery Programme (at the Arts Council of England). The Mondriaan Foundation awarded Autograph funding for the Netherlands-based artist Annabel Howland. The exhibition also received in-kind sponsorship from Photobition, for the fabrication of Ingrid Pollard's work, and from Katz Pictures for all our image duplication. S.T.I. was made possible by an R&D grant from SciArt (www.sciart.org/) and is supported by The Institute of Digital Art and Technology (www.i-dat.org).

I would also like to thank the Bermondsey Artists Group (David Allen, Jane Barnes, Francis Coleman, Steve Dunn, Tony Fleming, Malcolm Jones, Peter Maclean), Dominic Moore and the technical support team at Leeds, Renée Musai, Eileen Perrier and Mark Sealy at Autograph. I am also grateful to Jorella Andrews for producing such a considered text for this publication.

Jananne Al-Ani's thoroughness whilst working on both the exhibition and publication has proved to be an invaluable support. Finally, I would like to thank all the artists for their contributions and for their commitment to the project.

Richard Hylton September 2001

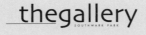